FINDING POSITIVITY

IN THE MIDST OF

NEGATIVITY

AYOKUNLE ADESINA

Finding Positivity In The Midst of Negativity
Copyright © 2024 by Ayokunle Adesina.

MILTON & HUGO L.L.C.
4407 Park Ave., Suite 5
Union City, NJ 07087, USA

Website: *www. miltonandhugo.com*
Hotline: *1- 888-778-0033*
Email: *info@miltonandhugo.com*

Ordering Information:
Quantity sales. Special discounts are granted to corporations, associations, and other organizations. For more information on these discounts, please reach out to the publisher using the contact information provided above.

Library of Congress Control Number: 2024910454
ISBN-13:   979-8-89285-110-7   [Paperback Edition]
                    979-8-89285-111-4   [Digital Edition]

Rev. date: 05/17/2024

CONTENTS

—The more fear you entertain, the more trouble you are bringing on yourself, the more likely you are to fail; and this is not a curse.

INTRODUCTION

A big thank-you to my family and friends who encouraged me in my time of hardships. Especially to my wonderful family who stuck with me during every difficult situation and trial I have been through in life. I cannot give enough thanks to the Great Man upstairs for giving me the opportunity to be able to write this book in my life. I had started to write initially but took a different decision not writing a book. Now, the Lord had been laying it in my heart that I must finish this book after taking several breaks and contemplating whether to write this book or not. Glory be to the Almighty Living God, who has still made me to be alive today. You will find that every issue you face in life has a solution to it whether you like it or not. Being the last of six in my family, I had the opportunity of being spoiled and spoiled to the extent that everything was done and given to me until I went to college and started figuring things out on my own. The year I came to America was August 1996, which I do remember vividly with my dad, mum, and brother. I want to say a big thank-you to my dad and mum who made me who I am today, and most especially to God.

You will encounter one problem or another in your life, in fact if you have not already had so. Everyone will carry their own cross at some point in their life. How you deal or face your problem will determine how strong you are in, and how you can face adversity in times of trouble or hardships. It is written in the Bible that we will face trials and tribulations. "But be of good cheer, He has overcome the world" (John 16:33). Having said all these, let me dig into my life's story and hope the reader of this book can get the most out of this book. What you encounter in this book and in my life's personal story, I encourage you to incorporate the advice, guidelines, and counsel that I have shared with you all. It may be useful at some point in your life, and you will remember such and such advice was given to you.

Let me start with a brief introduction about my medical condition. I was diagnosed with high blood pressure when I was at the age of eighteen, during trials for a basketball team at Widener University. More than a hundred million Americans are living with high blood pressure. Little did I know I had developed hypertension, should it be not for the physicals I had during that time. I had made several doctor's visits due to my blood pressure, and different medications have been changed for different reasons. Many Americans could have been living with this condition without knowing it, so it is important that one checks it regularly. Also, during one of my visits, I had been told I have an enlarged heart, which may have been the reason or what contributed to the blood pressure. Also shortly after the time I was diagnosed with hypertension, I had a condition in which I was sleeping for days with no underlying reason. In fact, this was not a normal condition and had my family worried. In fact, this type of condition—for a person to be sleeping most of the days out of twenty-four hours for almost a week— had not been known to the doctors.

After being to so many hospital visits, still, they could not diagnose the problem or give it a name. I thank the Lord that the sleeping issue had stopped many years ago. I find it absurd that anyone will be sleeping for days with no reason. During this abnormal state of sleeping for days, I would find out that I had cravings for different kinds of food—e.g., pizza, Chinese food, which I found to be strange. Lo and behold, this issue of sleeping was over many years ago. That will be one of the miracles that the Lord had done in my life. I want to encourage you, whatever situation you may be going through in life, there's always a solution for it. Anyone could have seen this kind of condition before in which they were sleeping and felt like they were in a different state of mind.

Another strange medical encounter I had was the issue of gout, which is a painful form of arthritis. This happens when there is too much uric acid in your blood and it forms a flare-up when the uric acid reaches a certain level. It usually hits the joints of the left or right big toe. This gout condition has happened to me on a number of occasions, and they were all painful experiences. I can clearly attest that anyone with all these conditions might have thought of suicide. Many people may not know how to deal with situations like this. The condition of my gout was so painful and hurtful that I had bad thoughts going through my mind, like my leg to be cut off. Ideally, one should be thinking positive thoughts and not negative ones. The first time I had the flare-up, it was so severe I had no idea what was going on; and eventually, I had to go the emergency room. Little did I know it was my first gout attack. I'm sharing all these experiences so one can know the pain one goes through in the hurdles of life. When any individual goes through challenges of life, it will only build you up and make you stronger so that when any challenge or adversity arises, you certainly know how to deal with them. Like I just mentioned, people may not be tough enough when they face certain challenges at what life throws at them.

Another interesting highlight that happened in my life was when I was on the plane on my trip from Nigeria. I was really sick during that trip to the extent that I was throwing up. The pilot had asked that a doctor should make himself available to a passenger. However, I did not receive any medical treatment during that flight. But upon my arrival, I had some people waiting for me to ask a few ridiculous questions, such as what country I was coming from, whom I associated with, what kinds of food I ate, and so on. It was only God that had his touch upon my life during that trip because I had some negative thoughts in my head. Every situation I had been through, it has been God that had brought me out of that situation. I have a message to the reader of this book: no matter what situation you may be going through, God has a solution for each and every problem you are facing. It may be that your issue is not being solved on time or you are not receiving your miracle early enough, I want you to know that if you stick through it or you are being patient enough, you will surely receive your miracle in due season. Most people get worried or even depressed when things are not going their way, which is a natural thing to do. But worry will add no single thing to your solutions; it will only add problems and get worse.

1

NOT GIVING UP AND BELIEVING IN YOURSELF

It was a nice, warm, and cloudy night in Cleveland, Ohio. The date was middle of May 2005. I was celebrating my last day of finals exam. I decided to go to a bar with a friend, and unfortunately, I let the celebration get out of hand. I acted like how other young people would—go out to the clubs and bars and having fun. It is the typical college norm that students engage in. On that faithful day, the last thing I remembered was driving and hitting a parked motorcycle. And lo and behold, it was an off-duty police officer that was hit. Oh boy, and reality did not hit me until I arrived at the place where people get locked up. After hitting the police officer, I recall a witness yelling the word *stop* right there because I was trying to run away. Get away, but to where? Trying to escape after I had hit an individual. It didn't occur to me what I was doing because I was still intoxicated.

Few minutes later, two police officers arrived, and I was asked to recite the letters from *A* to *Z* and recite the numbers from 1 to 10. After that, I was given a breathalyzer, in which I failed. Unlike most people, I wasn't in handcuffs; and next, I was booked in the county jail. There, once I arrived at the station, I had my picture taken for the initial booking, was asked what happened before my possessions were taken, and was escorted to the jail cell. I had no clue how long I was going to be there. The only thing I knew was that I was depressed because I did not belong in there. I cried, cried, cried, and prayed. My family did not know where I was until they called a friend on campus and informed my family of my whereabouts. I was there for almost a week—five days to be precise. During my stay at the jail, I met different kinds of people. Some were arrested for all kinds of issues. I craved for food when I was there. Breakfast was served around 5:00 a.m., lunch was ready around noon, and dinner was served anytime between 5:00 and 6:00 p.m.

What happened to me was beyond a miracle. It was a miracle for me and also a miracle for the police officer that was hit and didn't die. Because if he did, it would have been a whole different story. Before the trial began, there were series of prayers that were held on my behalf, and the Lord answered their prayers. If I didn't get out of prison, I felt something bad might have occurred to me, or I was thinking to myself, *Is this the end of my life?* I didn't know God had a better plan for me. After my trial date and after my release, what's next for the young college student? I was working at FedEx as a package handler. Well, that ended my career there. During this incident and the court cases, one of the consequences that resulted on this particular case was that I couldn't drive for a period of five years, which was really a period of me being patient and just waiting on the Lord. I knew the Lord definitely had a plan for my life. Five years is a really a long time one couldn't drive, and it was very frustrating. But I certainly learned one thing—that patience pays off no matter what you are going through in life. How will I be getting to work, interviews and my appointments? Lo and behold, those period of five years went by really fast; glory be to God most high. It is a difficult thing and frustrating task to find a company or a job that will hire someone with a felony case. I was charged with two counts of felonious assault. I applied for a lot of jobs daily but no result. As we all know, most companies do require a background check before they hire an employee. Since most companies require background checks, I have to keep fighting to get the dream job. It has been nine years since the incident occurred, being denied in so many places, and I am confident that I will rise and make it to the top. Every day is a new day, and each day is a miraculous day. During my course of fighting in the troubles of this life, Uber granted me employment as a driver, in which they do regular background checks. And suddenly, they ran background check on my Uber platform and found that my background wasn't clear. Well, I didn't let that trouble me. I knew that every adversity in life makes me stronger, and I can face any challenge that comes my way. I discovered that in life, there are many issues and trials that people face, but others overcome easily while others let the worries of this world overtake them. To the reader of this book, whatever situation you may be facing, be positive and stay strong and believe that you are an overcomer.

Few months after I was granted a greenlight to be an Uber driver, I gained another employment with Southwest Laboratories. I was fortunate that background check wasn't done on me; otherwise, I would not have been blessed with that job. There, my job title was a billing support specialist. The job lasted about seven months before most people in the company were laid off. During the time I was working there, I developed several health issues. Apart from the high blood pressure, I had a situation in which I had atrial fibrillation, which was a one-time condition and then went away after a few weeks. The cause of this, I did not know. Another condition I encountered was called gout, which is a form of arthritis commonly found in old people that majorly attacks the left or the right foot. I was really troubled and visited the emergency room about three times. My right foot was in severe pain, and I was given a few medications for the treatment. I do not want to remember the situation because it was a painful experience. The gout later reoccurred almost a year later, about the same time frame. I believe it was during the Fourth of July weekend. How ironic could that be? I though the alcohol was the cause for gout condition. I was forced to stop drinking alcohol and start eating healthy in order to maintain a healthy lifestyle. You may be going through some issues or know someone who is going through a tough time in life, please be encouraged and do not be discouraged.

I moved to Dallas, Texas, in May 2013 and have never had a full-time job since then. I have been going from job to job but never had the opportunity to work for a long time. After working at a lab company for few months, I had to wait about five months before securing my next job. I had to take a job as a caretaker. But before getting this job,

I was offered a temp job with a temporary agency, which lasted about five weeks. The same day that job ended was the day I was called about a caregiver Job. You may see this as an ordinary thing or no big deal. But it's actually a big deal. Many people are looking for opportunities like this, but to no avail. That's why you must thank God in whatever situation you are. This must be a blessing of God, having to lose a job in one day and securing another job the same day. This is one reason why I said my life is filled with miracles.

Many people are going through life depressed, hopeless, or even miserable due to one situation or another. I want you to know that there is someone out there who can rescue you from out of all your troubles. His name is Jesus, or Yahweh. He is the Miracle Healer, also known as Master Jesus. You may be going through a financial meltdown in your life, family, your marriage may not be working out as you thought it would, or your life may be full of a zigzag rides. I don't know what situation you are going through today, but I know one thing's for sure: when there is life, there is hope. I have been involved in a few occasions when I thought that I wasn't going to make it through life. Here I am today, hale and hearty. I definitely know that someone reading this short book will be blessed in all areas of life. Listen, don't quit in whatever situation you are and keep hoping for the best. You may have tried this or that career, failing in your businesses, or nothing may seem to be working out—just keep hanging on tight and keep believing that your miracle is around the corner. Perhaps you may have been scammed in one area or another. God will surely repay you multiple-fold.

As a master's degree holder, you would expect someone like me to be working in a big or a well-known company. That is not always the case. In fact, I'm not one of the smartest or brightest individual in the world. I have to admit that it takes me time to understand things or grasp materials. But eventually, I still understand or grasp the material or the subject. I am glad I made it through school, almost never graduated university and master's. In a nutshell, I had almost flunked out of my graduate school. I was given a letter that I would be sent out from the school, and I was placed on academic probation. I was on the verge of pulling out of the school, but suddenly, I had the courage to move on because I had only two classes remaining for graduation. How I pulled it out was a miracle and beyond my expectation. I myself could not even explain it, and it was beyond my situation.

It was during one of my last classes that a miracle happened. Had I gotten a C or lower, I would not have been able to graduate. Then maybe an appeal process would follow, or I might have been expelled from the school. We were given a project in which two people were assigned to the task. Fortunately, my partner was more experienced than me in the subject area, and I was able to gain a few things from him. There were about six sets of two people in a group. Like I just mentioned, my partner was an individual that was gifted with thinking outside the ordinary and quite intelligent. That was the reason why we became first out of all the students in the class project and we won. Many people started out universities and colleges but are unable to graduate. I would like to encourage you today, the reader of this book. No matter what situation you are facing in life, be encouraged and do not be discouraged. Always have a positive mindset or a can-do attitude in life. Your business may be failing or may have already failed or close to doom, but you will definitely succeed in life if you do give up.

Always remain confident and be positive that your business will rise to the top and you will be victorious. If I can finish and have an MBA degree and was on the verge of total failure, that means that you can also do the same. Likewise, if you are failing or not doing so well in life, in a project, or in a class, there is still the possibility that you might finish or end up well. Let us take the example of Bill Gates. Before he started making it big and became wealthy, he failed a few times. In the early '90s, Gates and Paul Allen started a company called Traf-O-Data. The company was a failure, and they eventually shut it down after they recorded loss of over $3, 000. Had its first business not failed, he and his company would not be where they are today. What point am I trying to make here? We all, at some point in our business—if we want to start out a business and be successful at it—might fail a little or big before we come become successful. If we don't fail, then we won't learn from our past mistakes. I have had several failures or mishaps in my life, which made me become more proactive, watchful, and make lesser mistakes today.

GETTING SELF-CONFIDENCE

Having self-confidence is one of the most difficult things to achieve in one's practical daily living. I have lacked confidence most of my life, which contributes to my weakness. Lacking self-confidence is basically the ability when you don't trust in yourself and lacks the skill in decision making. When you lack confidence, you don't have the ability to accomplish anything, and you start to feel worthless. It can affect you in your daily affairs and to accomplish tasks. I have come to the conclusion that I have been living in bondage of fear for more than fifteen years. I find it very difficult to accomplish tasks, some simple and some not to simple. In fact, this has affected me during some interviews and want to say this has contributed to me securing a job. When one is confronted with fears and doesn't know how to proceed in life, it creates a big problem and or issue within oneself and doesn't allow one to accomplish some easy tasks. Most people who have succeeded in life have a high level of confidence and that has made them to be successful at whatever they do. Creating fear within yourself is one of the greatest negativity that can happen to one, and you put yourself in bondage once you allow that fear to set in. So how do you gain confidence? By trusting in yourself and believing that you can do whatever you set yourself out to do. Now this doesn't come easy, but by trusting and believing in yourself, you can become great in life. Bill Gates had the confidence when he invented Microsoft. Alexander Bell believed in himself when he created the first telephone. The Wright brothers believed in themselves when they invented the first aircraft. Self-confidence starts with you and your mind. When you have confidence, you can do anything and be on top of your game. When there is self-confidence, you can talk confidently in front of groups, do presentations comfortably, talk boldly in front of large crowds, and do well on any interviews you may have.

The first problem starts within you. When you think you can achieve something in life, no matter how difficult it is, then you can do it. If you don't believe or trust in yourself, you cannot achieve something or get anywhere in life. It is a difficult thing to be very dedicated in life, but you have to pursue your dreams and your vision to the fullest.

Many people start on goals, projects, or some tasks and end up only to back out without completing the task. They feel the task is too complex for them or is unachievable, so they take the easy way out by bolting away or abandoning the task. You may not get anywhere in life or just be going in circles all over again. To the reader of this book, I encourage you to start that school you've been wanting to start; I encourage you to start that training or course you have been wanting to start a long time ago. I plead with you not to give up in whatever task or project or training you want to do. I started writing this book some few years back. Now, I have decided that it is time to take the bull by the horn. It was a real challenge to put this book in writing, like I just mentioned, instead of procrastinating for a long time. This is the time I had to write this book, during the time of the pandemic—a time when everyone had to relax and take a break from their work environment and go into isolation, a time of meditation and everyone making the best use of their time. The time to write this book couldn't come at a much better time as this. Now is the time to finish what you have started. Procrastinating or delaying things almost always comes with negativity. When you delay things, there's at least some kind of negativity attached to it.

2

GOING IN THE RIGHT DIRECTION

Most people wander about life going in the wrong direction, but why? People go around in circles not getting to their destinations in life, just like an animal wandering around the bush not knowing his or her destination. A lot of people today are not successful in their marriages, their jobs, careers, etc. When you don't know what you want to do in life, it becomes a big problem; and you just go around instead of you going from A to B to C to D, people go from A to B back to A, the starting point again. Life sometimes doesn't give you what you deserve, but you have to be courageous and say to yourself that you will make it in life. Ask yourself questions: What am I here on Earth for? What is it I like doing? What is my purpose in life? When you ask these questions and ask God to give you a change of heart, you have taken a big step of change toward your life.

As you have read, I have been through a lot of tough situations in life. I have been perplexed but not broken down. God has given me the grace to rise up and fight the battles of life. When you have a sense of direction in life, things will begin to work out good for you, and things will be easy for you. You may begin to achieve the things you did not achieve before. We can see that most successful people have focus and direction in life. Many people wake up roaming around in circles, not having a sense of direction. When you don't have a sense of direction in life, then your life becomes meaningless. You need to know where you want to go in life and not waste time.

Through life's experiences, I have noticed that a lot of people waste time in choosing their life partners, their careers, starting out a business, and implementing ideas. Time is one of the most important resources we can utilize on this earth. When you utilize your time wisely and ask God for a sense of direction, your life will become meaningful and you will live a life fulfilling a purpose. Another question you can ask yourself is "What do I like to do or what are my hobbies?" A lot of people are in the wrong profession or wrong field, and they are doing something totally different from what they are called to do. If you know what you like doing or take passion in your tasks, it can become your profession in life. For example, some people like cooking, but maybe they don't want to take that route of being a chef, while God has chosen that career path as being a chef for them. Some are called to be pastors, and they have not yielded to God's voice yet. To the readers of this book, whatever situation you find yourself, don't give up. Always strive and get to the next level. Sam Walton, Jeff Bezos, Warren Buffet, Bill Gates, Steve Jobs, Michael Jordan didn't become millionaires or billionaires overnight. They achieved what they wanted through hard work, and the end result is success. Although they definitely had some rough patches or stumbling blocks on the way ahead, but they pulled through. These are the things that makes one tough and makes them scale through any situation one might face in life. No one will scale through life easily or will become wealthy overnight by having no failures or roadblocks. It may seem frustrating and depressing after waiting so many years for that particular job you wanted or that field you wanted to work in. Don't worry, I have good news for you. A miracle is coming your way soon. Just believe and say. "Thank you, Lord. Thank you, Lord for the new job and miracle you have coming my way."

I found out that many people get frustrated when things are not going their way. In fact, some of them get angry or mad at God. God is surely not sleeping. You ought to thank him for being alive, giving you good health, being able to walk, not being in a hospital. We often lose our focus in life when things are not going our way. Some people even get to the point of committing suicide. That thought should never happen to any individual. If you are going through any issues or problems in life, my recommendation is to visit your local support groups and seek help. It saddened my heart when I heard on the news that a teenager committed suicide when he faced losses of thousands of dollars in the stock market. Had he had some patience, the outcome might have turned positive for him, or things might have turned around good for him. Things would have definitely worked out for him if he had a personal relationship with God. I can't know whether he had believed in God or not, but more than likely if he did, God would have spoken to him to be patient and worked out things in his favor. Another important thing is to seek God's face and ask him to help you. Every problem or difficult situation you have is in the Book of Life (Bible). It is an instructional book that makes us learn and live life according to God's plan or will. Matthew 11:28 says, "Come to me all ye that labor and are heavy laden, and I will give you rest." Jesus assures us that he will give us rest. *Heavy laden* simply means "carrying a heavy load." When you carry a heavy load, you start to worry and cannot focus.

Whenever you are in trouble, it is always important to seek God's face. It is easy to get carried away with the troubles of this world. It says in the Bible that we will face trials and tribulations, but be of good cheer, he has overcome the world. Many people turn to man to help instead of God. It is true that man can be your closest friend, but there is one that can never disappoint—his name is Jesus. He is always there when you need him. The Lord says we should ask him anything according to his name and he will do it.

Like I mentioned earlier in this book, I may not be the brightest person in the world. But one thing I do believe is that each brand-new day sets a tone for you to get better in life. Your situation today doesn't determine who you will become tomorrow. You may be a beggar or be very poor, but God may turn your situation around overnight, only if you believe in yourself and God. What does it mean to be going in the right direction in life? It means you are going in the way God has called you to go. It simply means you are being called to do what you are called to do. Many people go astray in life because they do not have an understanding of what God has called them to do. Find a passion of what you like doing the most and stick to it. It means you have a passion for your life and know exactly what you want to do in life. Going in the right direction means being called by God to lead you in the right way and not going astray. I must say I am fortunate to have a job of my desire—not a profession I wanted to do at my youth but what I had passion for as I grew older. Having worked at a fast-food restaurant as my first job, it is a great privilege to be working as an SAP consultant at the time I was writing this book. I had almost given up due to disappointments after doing many interviews. Nearly at the edge of my giving up studying to be a consultant, I received my miraculous breakthrough.

My first SAP consultant job was in Milwaukee, Wisconsin. I give all the glory to the Almighty God because I wasn't expecting the job. Well, to my surprise, the job didn't go so well. I lost the job only after two and a half months. Not until two months after, I received an offer letter for yet another SAP consulting role in Tuscaloosa, Alabama. I would like to tell you that whatever you are going through, there is always a way out.

GIVING THANKS IN ALL THINGS

You may be wondering, "How will I pay this bill, how will I pay that bill? How will I pay that school loan? How will I pay that car insurance? How will I pay that hospital bill?" Well, I have good news for you today: you don't have to worry. As long as you have life, there is hope for the living. The Bible says in Philippians 4:19, "But my God shall supply all your needs according to his riches in glory by Christ Jesus." Amen. I have been through fire and been through a lot in life, so I am privileged to walk you through life's experiences and give you the daily dose you need in your daily lives or whatever you may be going through. I would like you, the reader of this book, to know that tough times don't last forever, tough people do. You may be doing the job you don't like or not even working at all. I have another good news for you: your new job is coming soon. Never give up. Always give thanks in whatever situation you find yourself in. Not having a job is quite distressing and maybe depressing sometimes, but you must never give up. You should be thankful you have a place to live, clothes to wear, food to eat, a car to drive. Only an ungrateful person will not be thankful for the good things they have. When you are thankful and are persistent in whatever situation you're in, then suddenly, things will begin to work your way.

As a conclusion to this chapter, when I say give thanks, I mean give thanks to the Almighty God who created you and who gave you air to breathe. I have written in the first chapter about how I got diagnosed with hypertension. In addition to the diagnosis, I have also had the following conditions in my life: atrial fibrillation, gout, UTI, kidney disease (second stage). Having these conditions doesn't mean I will go about life feeling depressed. No, things don't work that way. Instead, I will give thanks to the Lord for healing me of all my ailments and diseases. Like I mentioned earlier, one needs to be grateful in all situations; no matter if you had an accident or you're sick. It may be difficult to give thanks when you're sick or when in the hospital. But it is when you are giving thanks that the Lord Almighty will heal you. Paul and Silas were giving praises and singing when the chains suddenly fell off from them in prison.

3

PANDEMIC ERA

A s we all know, we are living in a time of despair and fear. In the Covid-19 or coronavirus time, this is one of the worst economic and depressing times not only for America, but for the whole world as well. I'm amazed by the world's stunning reaction of this pandemic. The whole setting of the world seemed like a movie with different parts to it, yet I seemed very perplexed watching people living in fear. However, I cherished the idea that people are living normal lives instead of isolating and living a life of fear and bondage, which could end up in depression. When people are living in fear and confusion daily, they are forgetting that there is a God, a God above all principalities and powers. Many individuals forget that there is a God above everything, a God that can heal all sicknesses and diseases. The media, television have even made it worse by telling us the number of casualties daily and people that have gotten infected. Oh, how I wish people can be positive and encouraging in such a times as this. There is a simple formula we need to know and apply it to our daily lives. Negative confession brings negative actions, or negative thoughts produce negative confessions, which in turn lead to negative results. When you ponder on negative things, negative or bad things begin to happen to you in your lives.

Unfortunately, I listened to the newscasters and they mentioned that the virus will come to Alabama, where I was living at the time, and it eventually did. Little does the world know that if we confess positive things, we will achieve positive results by all means.

Now, people began to rush to the stores and started buying all sorts of food stuff, toilet papers, napkins, and water, etc. There was a panic rush for all these things because the world did not believe in God. That is what it simply boils down to. If there were no state of emergency, the world would not be panicking and buying things. This chain of events that occurred should make people think in a whole new different way. There is a connection to what happened, which is connected spiritually. You can only see it if you are spiritually deep or sound.

I myself might have been a victim of the virus. This could have been, as I am not 100 percent sure, as I felt some of the symptoms that some people were feeling during the era of Covid-19. It was essential and was critical that people take the precautions very seriously. I had symptoms such as extreme fatigue, slight cough but nothing severe, and sore throat, or at least felt like something was stuck in my throat and felt really uncomfortable. I do not know for sure that I experienced this because maybe I did have the virus and it went away, or maybe I just entertained fear in my mind and I was thinking about the virus.

Many of us entertain fear and anxiety in our minds throughout our daily lives. In fact, the first thing we do when we get up in the morning is to start thinking about the deadly virus or about the bills we have to pay, about our health, about our family, about our jobs—whether we will lose it or not—about that spouse you are looking after. You may have been wondering, "How can I stop entertaining fear or worry in my life?" One thing you can do is to pray that God would remove fear from your mind. You may not be a Christian, but I encourage you to meditate on this scripture. In 2 Timothy 1:7; it says "For God has not given us a spirit of fear, but of power, and of love and a sound mind." When you read scriptures like this, you will begin to see things will begin to work out for you in your favor. Also in times like this of the pandemic, I find it necessary to encourage one another and your family. Another good scripture to meditate on and to think upon is Isaiah 41:10. It says, "Fear not, for I am with thee: be not dismayed; for I am thy God; I will strengthen thee, yea I will help thee." When you think about and read Bible verses like this, you will overcome fear with time. I, however, do not intend to write this book as a Christian book; but in times like this, when there is so much fear and worry going on in the world, I have no choice but to chip in and help those who are worried and those who live in fear in every day of their lives.

In honesty, I was really worried I had the coronavirus. Immediately, my mind started to entertain all kinds of negative thoughts. On the eve of April 1, I felt feverish for a few minutes and had shortness of breath for about ten seconds. Few minutes later, I was back to my normal self. Could it being the thoughts that I had entertained myself with days earlier started to sink in and I started to feel that way? Be careful what you wish for because you might get it. Now I had to change my mindset and started to think positively. I had to do away with negative thoughts and start to meditate on different Bible scriptures, and I began to feel better and get well. My dear friends, I have good news for you today. Don't let that situation you are in weigh you down. Do not be discouraged, but be encouraged. Your friend might have a better job than you; he might be driving a Benz, BMW, or a very nice and exclusive car. Don't worry or be jealous. Rejoice with your friend because in due time, your season of harvest will come. You will get your own luxury car or that job you have been waiting for. You can write it down as long as you don't give up and as long as you believe in yourself that you can make it.

It had to take a lot of courage for me to write this book about my life because I started writing so many times and left it because I wasn't motivated anymore. Suddenly, I had the courage to begin writing once more and especially during the time of stay-at-home order.

As a matter of fact, not that I am eager or happy that this pandemic occurred, but it has definitely made me change my mind about life. I began to look at life on a whole new different dimension. I began to see that people's attitude began to change; people began to cut off friendships with other people. People that were close to God did not get close to him anymore. I saw a lot of people's mindset were fixed on different things; they were eager to get back to things that they normally do on their regular lives. I have come to realization that people need a break from stressful lives; they need a break from their tedious, complex and so-called stressed-out lives. Everyone needs a long break and a change in their lives. We cannot blame God; however, for this kind of situation, a lot of businesses were hurt, thousands or millions of people lost their jobs, stock markets collapsed, thousands of people died. It just couldn't get any worse. But one thing to keep in mind is that as long as you have your job and as long as you have life, you should be grateful for all of this.

One thing is certain: we live in a world of negativity by the media and TV and other news. They bombard us with all kinds of negative news in our environment. So many individuals are forced to believe the news that we are being fed. Like I mentioned earlier, despite the news that slows everyone's daily lives, this period was to enjoy your friends and family at home. I believe people will also and should learn important habits of sanitizing and good personal hygiene. One way to be positive in this kind of environment is that you are working, you have life, and you have your family or someone to talk to. On the negative side, a lot of people are lonely, are in the hospital, are depressed, have lost loved ones—some are in incarcerated or some people are just no more. Every day, you wake up; you need to have a positive aspect on life and declare to yourself that this is a great day. A lot of people wake up feeling depressed and sad every day. No wonder there is a rising suicide rate in America. Some people have lost all hope, forgetting that your problem can be solved one day. When you think all hope is lost, don't give up. There is a solution to your problem or issues in life. The first step is to believe in yourself that you can do anything because if you don't believe in yourself, then fear sets in. The second step is to recognize what is going wrong or what went wrong. The third thing is to take corrective actions or measures so you don't repeat the same mistakes again—although some people learn by making a lot of mistakes over and over again.

During this pandemic era, we find that the best often comes out to people who made the best out of this Covid situation. It could have been the perfect time for you to start a business or to look into an activity you love doing as a career or something you had wanted to do a long time ago. It could also be some kind of training or skilled work. My dear friends, do not let this time and opportunity pass you by. We don't often get this kind of opportunity but maybe once in a lifetime. It may very well be during this time. Some took advantage of the downtime and became very wealthy. But you should make the best use of it and make something positive out of this pandemic. Some may say they have no help or Money, while others are still making it big time. You need to think and find a way to make it happen. I believe you do not have any excuse to lose. Thousands have used this opportunity to start some kind of business—it could be an online business, it could be a business of selling masks. Many individuals have started the business of selling masks during this period. I may sound repetitive and too forceful, but those who take to advice and take heed usually become successful; those who do not give up, distinguish themselves and are patient are those who come out on top. I truly believe that God does test and is testing our faith and our beliefs not to give up in certain situations because in our struggles and perseverance come the best out of us. When we know how to act in certain situations or go through the hurdles in life, that fully prepares us for the next best test or life's hurdles. Do not become discouraged in whatever situation you are facing in life, and I will continue to say this repeatedly.

I have given you many advice in this book. One is to be calm in whatever situation you are or find yourself in. When you do this, you begin to discover that certain things begin to work out for you. I am not asking you to change your religion or pray a lot. But for me, what works is that I believe in God, have faith, and pray. What works for me may not work for you, but what you certainly need to do is to have faith, believe in God Almighty, and do away with fear as much as possible. I am still struggling in this area of fear for many years now. A very vivid example is that my boss may be walking across the aisle or close to my desk and fear suddenly grips me, or whenever I hear a noise or something drops on the floor, fear suddenly grasps me. However, I am trying my possible best for fear not to grip me. But this issue has been going on for more than ten years. I do try and encourage myself that I need to get over this fear or being afraid and replace it with being confident. That is one of my biggest weaknesses in life, and I know I will definitely overcome it sooner than later.

If you don't know how to control the fear within you or it's almost impossible one can control it, one will almost have issues or troubles in their daily lives or their careers. The more fear you entertain, the more trouble you are bringing to yourself, the more likely you are to fail; and this is not a curse. Being entangled with fear means that one is in a bondage, or at least you have been in that bondage of fear for a long time. When you entertain fear or worry, you automatically assume that you can't accomplish things, and this revolves around your mind regularly. For you to overcome this, you must be willing to let go of the fear, start thinking positively, and let go of some things in your life. To the readers of this book, if some of you are dealing with this issue of fear, it is time to be set free and be free indeed.

CHAPTER

4

DOING THE RIGHT THING AND HELPING OTHERS

You should always try and get in the attitude of doing the right thing every time and try helping others. It may be difficult, but one should try and be a blessing to others. It is when you go out of your way to help others when the blessings come back to you. I have made it a point earlier: it is essential to be giving or helping others. It says in Matthew 7, that when one gives, it shall be given back unto you with good measures. It's necessary and essential for one to give with a cheerful heart. If, indeed, you give grudgingly, you may end up not receiving or getting little back.

One place you can start giving is to the less privileged. There are many individuals that are less privileged than you worldwide or globally. When you look at the statistics of the people that are malnourished, poor, or less privileged, you can see that we have close to 15 percent in America and in other countries, especially in African countries. When you do this, you separate yourself from most people that are doing less in acts like this or don't give at all. Helping others, doing a random act of kindness, giving to the charity, serving in your local church are all great examples of helping people. When you show this acts of kindness, it always comes back to you in a good way one way or the other. Many people find it difficult to assist others due to the fact that they don't feel they should and possibly due to their financial status. But be helpful to others, no matter what you face in life. A good place you can start giving can be in your local community; you can do so by volunteering and joining local groups or by joining support groups. If you can't give money, you can give part of your time by helping others. You can help others during a time of hardships or a time of tough times; although money will definitely be a good source of help to others. Whatever you do, whether good or bad, it always comes back to you one way or another. If you give help or render assistance to others, you always get blessed one way or another. If you commit a crime against others or you do evil things, karma always catches up to the person. I don't know if people have any sense of consciousness or any guilt during the process of committing their evil acts. But whatever bad things they do always catches up to them.

We can see a vivid and realistic example in our nation these days. Workers of the law system in this nation are not making good choices. For instance, we have the issue of the police officers being guilty of several crimes against the African Americans over the last few years. We can clearly see and conclude the issue of racial injustice against a certain ethnicity. This needs to stop, and we need the police force to start taking sensible actions and using good judgement in our community. We see things like this where the police officers are using wrong judgments, and it is rising in several of the states across the nation. Helping people that are in need or trouble is by no means an act of wrongdoing but an act of kindness, but remember that, when you do good, the good that you render will surely come back to you. I don't know what people feel in their hearts or mind when they see others suffering, and they are in a position to help but they didn't. Are you feeling any sense of doubt or being convicted in your heart that you should have assisted that individual? Are you having a regret that you didn't help that person on the road or help the homeless man asking for help? Are you having a sense of guilt or not letting go of the past that you didn't help that friend or that colleague or that brother because they have hurt you in the past and you haven't forgive them? Well, you need to let go of the past so you be free of yourself and move ahead in life. When you hold on to grudges or not forgive people, you are only hurting yourself and not the other party.

RELATIONSHIP OR MARRIAGE STRUGGLES AND FAILURES

To the reader of this book, you might be struggling through a certain relationship you are in or might be going through marriage issues. I have good news for you: you don't need to give up in that tough situation you find yourself in. You might have been enduring for a long time and just have a really miserable marriage. There is something called patience that you and your spouse can work out on. That is why you need to spend a lot of time with your spouse before settling down for marriage. You guys can work out things steadily, slowly and even attend counseling. But there is no guarantee all these can work out. The most important thing is to love and show patience and kindness to your spouse. You may have had many arguments caused by a very simple thing that can be resolved easily, and this could have happened many times. This is where the issue of patience comes in. You really need to have patience for one another and be able to tolerate each other. I'm sure you did not know it will be like this or tough like this, but I need to encourage you that things will certainly get better. The question is how long do you want to endure and stay in that relationship? I pray for you now that you find a quick fix or solution so that you may be better. Some of the things that cause marriage issues are finances. When the man or woman want to do things their own way or manage finances in the way they like, then it can cause several problems. One thing you both can do is to find a common ground and see where the issue lies and work things out. Maybe you are spending too much on groceries, maybe you both have a joint account and your husband or wife notices things you should not buy. Maybe the man or woman is not contributing enough in the household. This is where understanding comes in, and you both need to understand each other very well. As they say, Rome wasn't built in a day, nor did the athletes become superstars overnight. The best thing is to take time and study each other well. Issues could be worked out well amicably without having to fight over several things.

Another thing that could marital issues is in the area of sex. Your husband or wife could not be in the mood for sex at nighttime or during the morning while you may be not. It may also be possible that the partner likes too much sex and the other person is getting tired of it. One should be able to do things in moderation. Or maybe your partner has denied you of sex in several months and you are possibly in the mood for it every time. Maybe you have gone somewhere else to cheat or look for love or maybe your wife or spouse has done the same. Once again, you need to have a common ground and strike a balance to resolve this issues.

Per adventure, you may have dated several men or women and you figured out that still you are in the wrong relationship, or you may have had several marriages that didn't work out. But have faith and be positive that things will still soon start working in your favor. One solution is that you need to endure and be patient so your situation will turn around for good. As long as you can work things out with your spouse, if that situation is workable. You definitely need to spend a lot time with your significant other before marriage because that is how you figure things out between both of you. I have seen or heard about couples that have been together for many years—for example five, ten, or even twenty years. People don't need to endure that long in that kind of relationships or situations, but they need to find a way out. On the other side, I have seen couples that have had exceptional or excellent relationships for a long time. Not so that they didn't have any issues, but they found a way to weather through the storms, stuck with each other, and be there for each other during the tough times. Some of you maybe in an abusive relationship and can't endure anymore. What I'm saying is that you don't need to endure in those kind of relationships. You need to seek help or advice or, most importantly, get out of that marriage. You do not need to keep enduring for years and years if things don't change.

WHY BAD THINGS HAPPEN TO GOOD PEOPLE

People always have the notion that bad things will never happen to them or they assume that bad things can't happen to them. Since you are not the one that created the heavens, the earth, and the universe. God allows good or bad things to happen to anyone. He is the giver of life and decides when he can take it away. He decides the number of years we spend on this planet. He can allow certain situations to happen to people, to test our faith or to see our reaction. A lot of good people have come and gone; relatives or close ones have asked the question "Why did this happen to this person?" or "Why did God allow him or her to be gone so soon?" We can't question God for whatever reason. He can make people live long, give good health to people, or one's life can be gone unexpectedly due to one reason or another. Like I just mentioned, we have quite a number of people on this earth that have gone early. For example, we have pastors that have died early due to one reason or another.

We can't say just because they are pastors or a reverend that all things will be well and rosy. Things may definitely go bad for them; they may be sick or God can allow them to go to heaven early. They do sometimes have their challenges during the course of the race on this earth just like any other human being. For example, Kenneth Hagin was a great man of God. In fact, he had died and rose up again. He was not a perfect man, but he definitely had the characteristics of God. Let's take another example of another set of people. Look at millionaires for instance. They too sometimes have their own struggles and issues in life. Just because they are considered millionaires doesn't mean they won't have their burden or problems in life.

CHAPTER

5

THE GOD FACTOR

et me say that we are living in this world by miracles of our Lord Jesus Christ; and one thing that is helping us for sure is the God factor. My fellow people, how did you think you got the job you were waiting for? How did you think your marriage worked out when you were in the midst of giving up? How did you think you survived that accident when your car was totaled? Do you think it was your making or doing? God still has a reason and a purpose for you being alive. That is why he kept you during your hardships and struggles. He said in his word that "he will never leave us nor forsake us." When you take care of God's business, God will take care of your business. When you had no money in your bank account or you were looking for jobs after your college education. You were toiling day and night and very frustrated. More than 50 percent of people go about in life aimlessly without God and not believing in him, thinking it's their own making or just not concerned about God. Or let me say they're not conscious that there is someone out there who can solve their life's issues or problems.

We can see how God has performed many miracles in the Bible. For example, we can see how he delivered Paul and Silas from the prison. They were held bound for offenses they did not commit. These two followers of Jesus were beaten with rods, and they were stripped off their clothing. At midnight, they were singing hymns, and suddenly, the chains fell off them. The same God that did it back then is still performing mighty miracles today. To the readers of this book, when you factor God into your equation, God will certainly take care of your life's problems. He is the same God that delivered me when I had accidents, when I was looking for jobs; he is the same God that delivered me countless times when I'm supposed to have been dead by now. He is the same God that changed my thinking when I had evil thoughts running through my mind when I lost more than $7,000 to a scamming company that promised us profits. After I found out it was a scam, I was severely depressed for days, and the Lord dug me out from the pit I was in. One thing I can assure you, if you don't give up in life, no matter what you are facing, you will definitely overcome all issues in life. You may have been waiting for a particular thing, job, or business to come through, and possibly waiting for years for this one thing. One thing I can assure you is that God is not sleeping. He will certainly make your dream come through. Perhaps he doesn't want you to have that thing at that particular time or delaying it for some other reason. When you look at Numbers 23:19, it says "God is not a man, that he should lie, neither the son of man, that he should repent: hath he said, and he not do it? Or hath he spoken, and shall he not make it good?"

Has God given you a promise in your life that he has yet to fulfill? And then nothing happened. Did your situation or circumstance get worse when you needed God the most? Did you misinterpret God's intentions? Where are God's blessings? God gave Joseph promise that one day that he would rule, but for the next thirteen years, everything went opposite for Joseph. He was sold into slavery, and his brothers hated him. As a slave in Potiphar's house, he was falsely accused of raping his master's wife; he was even thrown into prison and forgotten. Joseph didn't let the circumstances take ahold of his situation. He didn't allow bitterness, anger, or malice take control of his life or emotions. After all he went through, God blessed him, turned his life around, and made him a blessing to others. Instead of using the delayed promise as an evidence against God, he kept believing and didn't let his faith wither. He kept trusting God that something good would eventually happen to him, and the promise that God made will come to pass in his life. God had something big planned for him more than what he imagined. He was given the powerful position as the second commander in Egypt, and he was even Pharaoh's assistant. He even saved the lives of his whole family.

As we all know, a delay is not denial or does not necessarily mean we're being denied of our blessings. It is actually a process that something great is coming our way. It is definitely a time of preparing us for his promise. When we don't see God working in action, he may be preparing something great for us behind the doors. So I want to encourage you today: do not let your faith wither or do not be weary. I waited for up to five years before landing my first IT job after doing training and several interviews. I was in the process of switching career paths, but God had a better plan for me. It is better to be patient than ending up making the wrong choice or making a mistake. Just be patient; your breakthrough is around the corner.

I have been in many situations in life that almost broke me. But by God's grace, I am confident to say that nothing can move me; no trials or tough situation I come across can move be in life, nor will my faith definitely be shaken. There is a purpose and reason in what you are going through. Perhaps God is trying to correct your direction in life. It could be that he is using these trials to teach you to lean more on him. Trust his timing and strengthen your faith. You may be going through this or that because how you respond may influence others in their decisions to follow Christ. It is possible that wading through all this mess in your life will help you lead someone else through a similar circumstance later in their life's journey, and you will be a positive impact on them. Like Joseph, we may not see the purpose for our struggles right away until much later. But also like him, we should remain faithful and trust that God knows what is happening. He is surely cooking some delicious meal for us.

Try and compare your life now from back then—fifteen or twenty years ago. Were you not better off? You have learned quite a lot financially, spiritually, and you certainly will not make the same mistakes over and over again. In fact, you must begin to look at your life and say to yourself, you are a product of God and you are part of

God's factor. Because God is the reason why you're still alive today. He has the ultimate say in your life, whether you like it or not. It's the God factor that you have in you that's not making you to give up in life. It's that same factor that's making you push ahead in life and achieving that dream you had of becoming someone special. It's the God factor that you have that healed you of your sickness and your disease when you thought you were going to die. It's that same factor that kept you going in your darkest moments. It's certainly not by your doing or making, and you may have heard of this God that we speak of, but you may have been strong-headed or unwilling to believe and yield to him. Trust in him, believe in him, and he will make all your days to be prosperous even when you don't think so. It's the God factor that definitely has your back when your bank account is low.

BE CAREFUL WHO YOU ASSOCIATE WITH

In life, it is very important who you associate with. Don't think you know it all. It is important who you keep as friends. Who you keep as friends can break you or make you in a good way. Try as much as possible to associate with good friends and good people. The Bible says in Proverbs 13:20, "He who walks with wise men will be wise but the companion of fools will be destroyed." This simply means that if you walk with wise people and individuals full of wisdom, it is more than likely that you will pick some of their brains, and you can also learn things from them. We have seen, and it is a common theme that rich folks likely associate with rich people. You can never see or almost never see a wealthy man associating with a poor man. When you associate with people full of wisdom, it can also make you to be successful for life.

Be careful also not to associate with bad company. When you do associate with bad people, there is tendency that you become what they are or you do things that you normally don't do. For example, younger folks tend to be peer-pressured into doing bad things like smoking, drinking alcohol, having sex at a young and tender age. All these things tend to be youthful exuberance, and they don't normally see any wrong in that. That's why parental care is very crucial to people at a young age so when they grow up, they know the difference between right and wrong and also what kind of company they keep. Once these teenagers get hooked with bad company, it takes an impact on their life and health. They will become addicted to drugs for a long time, which impacts their immune system in the long haul. About 85 percent of high school students have felt peer pressure and about 10 percent of kids believed that peer pressure has never influenced them. In today's society, it is very difficult not to be peer-pressured. When you work with people of good character and wealthy friends, you can learn their work habits, their lifestyles, the way they make income; and you can try to make similar choices like them. You don't have to copy them exactly but try and act in a good manner as well. When one make bad choices in life, thank God for the rules and laws out there; one can get punished easily. When you run the red lights, when you speed too much, when you are driving drunk, you can get punished easily by the police officers or simply get a speeding ticket in the mail. When you do all these things, there are consequences for it. Likewise, when you are a good person in a society, when you give back to the community or when you make an impact in your state or society, you can get recognized for your wonderful acts or accomplishments.

CONCLUSION

I n summary, I hope you enjoy life to the fullest and enjoy what life brings you. You need to stick with the situation and hope for the best no matter the stage of life you're in, whether you are facing challenges or not. I have thrown what life has given me to you all in this short book, and I hope you take what advice this book has offered you with a heart of gratitude. I'm sure you've all experienced good, bad, and the ugly at one stage or another in your life. The key is to have patience if you have a certain goal you want to attain or you want a certain career you are struggling to achieve. Perhaps, if you are happy with yourself, keep pushing on and be on guard and alert for the enemy. Because he's looking to attack the successful ones and bring them down. Why must one be going through life depressed and down all the time? One should be living a life that is free of fear and free of worry. Like I mentioned to you earlier, one will go through a lot of tests and hassles in life. It is left to one how he handles the problems of life. Life will certainly give you what you deserve, but I promise you that things will certainly get better.

I am in a position to write about my issues in life and how it relates to what a lot of people are going through today in this world. One way or another, you need to find positivity in the midst of crisis you are in. Don't be discouraged, dismayed, but be encouraged for your testimony is right around the corner. There are a lot of people in this world that want to take shortcuts in life, and they don't understand that what goes around comes around. You may have been taking a lot of shortcuts in life, cheating or doing things that are not worthy. I have seen a lot of people struggle in life, and some people are just blessed by good fortune in life. For example, some people were born into a wealthy family so they may not have to struggle much in life, and that is why I am in a position to view and write about my life's story. Can you imagine what life would have been like without any struggles or hassles? Life would have been so much better, right? And everyone wouldn't have troubles, right? But right from the inception of this world from the garden of Eden from Adam and Eve, there were troubles since then, and it has continued up till today. The troubles of this world have started many decades ago and will still continue. Also, another piece of advice I give to my readers is to really be positive in life and distinguish yourselves in everything you do. I believe it's right not to imitate or copy others, and you should try and be creative in whatever you are trying to accomplish in life. Imitating others may lead to failures, confusions, and not knowing which way to go. It is best if you try to be unique in whatever you do, and you may even discover some new things in life.

I do hope you have really learnt a few things in the course of this book. It may be a very difficult thing to do to find happiness and positivity during your storms. But I do want to encourage you, if you hang in there and hang on tight, your breakthrough may be around the corner. It's a very difficult thing to do to be positive when you are going through storms. I can cite a very good example. I have been a victim of a scam when I and my older sister invested in bitcoins from a binary trading company. After the company promised that we will get thousands of dollars back after investing, in the end, it turned out to be a scam. It turned out to be nothing but empty promises from this particular company. After we invested close to $10,000, I was obviously not a happy person for days. I was just getting over it after about three days. But the empty promises I would always remember and will be careful in the future. One piece of advice I would like to give the readers of this book is to never be in a rush to do anything. If you are not sure about any action you want to undertake, I would like to encourage you to take your time, do your research, and ask a lot of questions from people who have been there before or have solid knowledge of what you want to do. I can assure you that if you take your time and do diligent research, you will never go wrong. Not taking your time, quickly jumping into things, and taking rush decisions can be very costly and could hurt you in the long run. It can be a very depressing, hurtful, and sad thing after you found out you are expecting profits and you get absolutely nothing back from them.

My fellow brethren, I wish you nothing but good luck in life's journey. In all you do, be steadfast, be truthful to yourself and others. Remember to be kind to other people, always be courteous, always try and work hard knowing that hard work, patience, and perseverance bring success and happiness. This book was written in the sincere hope that you can actually discover who you are, your true self, and also you can actually find positivity and happiness in the midst of negativity or your struggles and hardships. Many people fall into hardships at one point in their lives. The point is how to get out of your struggles. We can all find a positive mindset or try to be positive in whatever situation we find ourselves in. It may be a quite difficult thing to do, but in all honesty, one has to find a way to be happy and not show sadness or pain even when you are going through trials and tribulations. People could notice your face and your reactions when you go to events, church, and such. Remember that the Bible says in James 1:2–4 "My brethren, count it all joy when you fall into various trials, knowing that the testing of your faith produces patience. But let patience have its perfect work, that you may be perfect and complete, lacking nothing." I know it may be and it is a difficult thing to be happy or not to show sadness when one has lost a family member or someone close to you. That could be an exception, knowing that the grieving pain only lasts a while. I can relate to this, having lost one of my uncles last year. We certainly all felt the pain, and it lasted for a while. While these are normal things to go through in life, it will make one to be stronger and overcome similar challenges you encounter again the next time. You may have had a divorce or going through a job loss; it is certainly understandable to feel the pain and show emotions for some time, maybe weeks, months, or years. But the trials of your test will definitely bring the best out of you. The intent of this piece of work is to give you step-by-step and ideas how you can reach success and how you can come out of it all, and most importantly, how to reach your life's full potentials. Wishing you nothing but positive thoughts and best wishes in life's Journey.

www.ingramcontent.com/pod-product-compliance
Lightning Source LLC
La Vergne TN
LVHW011339080426
835513LV00006B/439